A recipe for dreaming

Also by Bryce Courtenay

The Power of One

Tandia

The Pitch

April Fool's Day

The Potato Factory

WRITERS' BLOC

THE READER IS ALWAYS RIGHT

A recipe for dreaming

Bryce Courtenay

Illustrations by Ann Williams

William Heinemann Australia

Published 1994 by William Heinemann Australia
a part of Reed Books Australia
35 Cotham Road, Kew, Victoria 3101
a division of Reed International Books Australia Pty Limited

Reprinted 1994, 1996, 1997

Typeset in Perpetua and Remedy
Designed and typeset by Mary Callahan
Printed and bound in Hong Kong

National Library of Australia
cataloguing-in-publication data:

Courtenay, Bryce, 1933–.
A recipe for dreaming.

ISBN 0 85561 549 4.

1. Self-actualization (Psychology). 2. Optimism. I. Williams, Ann, 1942–.
II. Title.

158.1

Introduction

One of the nicest things to happen to me after I'd written *The Power of One* is that it has become a book which young people seem to enjoy a lot. They write to me or they come to see me and the question I am most often asked is:

'Can you help me to decide what to do with my life?'

So I wrote this little book and quite a lot of people – not only young people – seemed to like it, even take courage from it. Authors are rather fortunate people, they are not really any wiser than anyone else, yet they get to have a say, even though they don't always deserve to be heard. It's a nice indulgence and here I am taking advantage of it.

In the first part of this book I have written about returning to the essential act of day dreaming. We need to dream, as a soaring imagination is the glue that keeps our soul from shattering under the impact of a prosaic world.

In the second part I've simply thrown in a few thoughts, questions really, that have occurred to me from time to time. The combination of learning to dream and getting into the habit of asking yourself questions is, I believe, the beginning of a way to live a happy and original life.

Then Ann Williams, who has been my friend for twenty years, came to the rescue of *A Recipe for Dreaming* by offering to illustrate it. As she has several times more talent as an artist than I have as a writer, I was totally delighted.

You see, if you don't care for the words, I know you'll take great delight in the pictures, which are very wise and gentle and say a great deal on their own.

Bryce Courtenay

Grabbing the moment

Birth—

Tic — Toc — Tic — Toc — Tic — Toc —

Death

She gave me a look of white hot apathy...

okay for you,'
she said, looking down at her hands resting in
her lap. 'You're clever. I can't tap-dance, I can't
dare my genius, I can't find any unknown paths
to walk, I can't even think of anything to dream
about. I get so bored thinking about myself, the
hands at the end of my arms rock me into a
stupor. My mind is manure.'

She paused and looked directly up at me.
'Quite frankly, Bryce, all this hopeful crap you
go on about makes me want to throw up
in your lap!'

Cloud drift

you remember
when you were a kid and you'd lie in the grass on
your back and watch the clouds scud above you
and dream of what you were going to be
when you grew up?

Well, what happened?

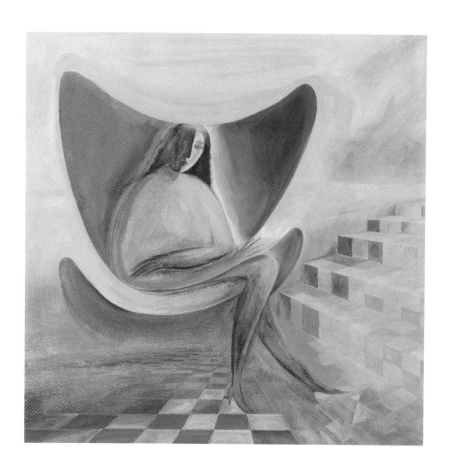

First things tomorrow

a comfortable
chair, close your eyes, put your hands in your lap
and start learning how to dream again. Dream for
five minutes. Dream about the past. Dream about
what you've already been. Repeat this the next
day and the next.

After some ten days you'll get the knack of
dreaming again. You'll begin to regain the long
lost art of dreaming. Then start dreaming
forward. Dream what has yet to be done.
Dream a direction for yourself.

The value-added you

There's you,
good old you, not too bad, not too good, safe, sure,
reliable, steady as you go. You.

A bit of a deterioration really from the perfect baby your
mother claims you were. What can you possibly add to the
sum of yourself that would make you love yourself more?

Not something for the kids, or your husband or wife, or your friends. No more self-sacrifice or feeling sorry for yourself. Add something that makes you more valuable and lovable to the person you talk to all the time.

Keep thinking for as long as it takes to find the value you want to add. Unless you're perfect already, it's generally not too hard to find at least one 'If only ...' You know, if only I had the time, money, education, intelligence, talent, I would ...

If you're going to add value to yourself you must make yourself the top priority. You are, after all, the most urgent project you can possibly undertake. Working on yourself is the single most rewarding thing you can do.

Eventually everyone you know will benefit hugely from the result.

Walking down the centre of the road

spent your life
walking down the centre of the road. You tell yourself
it's important to be safe. Security comes first. It's a
hard cruel world, so you'd better play it safe now
than be sorry later. Fools rush in ...

But nothing is more certain than that if you walk down
the centre of the road, you are going to be hit by the
traffic coming from both directions.

Playing it safe is the most dangerous thing
you can possibly do.

Dare your genius to walk the wildest unknown way

Go where you've never been before. Dream up a destination, a path to follow, a wildest unknown way, over rocks and scrag, across high hills where the winds bite cold with malice, through deep mysterious valleys where the wild things roar and echo and rumble and stamp and hiss great clouds of steam from their terrible huffing ways.

Dream the impossible dream and start walking towards it.

On the way you'll be beaten up, chewed, spat out, mauled, ripped apart, given up for lost. Quite soon you'll learn what it feels like to be beaten up, chewed, spat out, mauled, ripped apart and given up for lost.

This is called 'experience' and it's very, very valuable in life, because what you mostly learn from it is that you were more afraid of what *might* happen than what *did* happen. Most successful outcomes are achieved by calling a series of conventional bluffs.

One bright sunny morning you'll discover that the wild and unknown way you took is carpeted with moss and strewn with tiny flowers. It has become a familiar path, a well trodden direction which has put you miles ahead of anyone else and much, much closer to achieving your once impossible dream.

Get away from the bottom and the top
will take care of itself

isn't hard at the top.
It's easy. It isn't crowded and it's really quite civilised.
What's hard is the bottom. Down there you'll find one
hundred times more competition. Down there is where
people stand on your teeth so that they can get a firmer
foothold on the first rung of the ladder out of hell.

Why then is it that most people seem to be so afraid of
success that they'll do almost anything to avoid it?

You were not born empty

God formed you with
perfect feet and hands and a heart that beats non-stop,
sometimes for a hundred years. He made you complete.
Why then do you assume He made you empty?

He didn't, of course. You inherited a thousand generations of wisdom, skill, poetry, song, all the sunrises and sunsets of knowledge past. You are the sum of all of the people who went before you.

You are a refinery of inherited intellectual wealth. The full flood of antecedent wisdom is piped and stored within you – how to climb the highest mountain, slay the biggest monster, how to survive fear and how to summon your own courage and take pride in your wonderful intelligence.

Inside you are more possibilities than you could possibly use up in one lifetime.

If you can dream it, you can do it, because the instinctive knowledge of how to succeed is already programmed within you waiting to be turned on. Waiting to flow like a river as you come on stream.

When you're skating on thin ice you might as well tap-dance

your neck out, volunteer, have a go, reach out beyond your best performance and when you do, do so with style, *élan*, panache. You will learn more from a brilliantly executed failure than from a success planned within the dreary safety of what you already know.

Winning easy is boring, pointless work.

If you don't know where you're going, then how will you get there?

Make pictures in your mind. See the destination.
Imagine your arrival. Dream in perfect detail.
See yourself the way you want to be when you arrive.
See yourself arriving. Make yourself a road map
and study it every day until you know the way
and the destination by heart.

20,000 words a day
and most of them defamatory

We speak to ourselves all
the time. Most days we direct around 20,000 words
at ourselves. Of these nearly all are negative.
We keep feeding our minds with negative dialogue.
How long would you expect to keep a friend if
you did the same thing?

You *are* your own best friend. Start talking to yourself
nicely. Say kind things to yourself about yourself.
Believe. You'll be amazed at the difference it makes
to the person you know most intimately and
love the best.

The helping hands you're going to need in life are located at the end of your arms

yourself into your
own hands. Everybody has two. You can use them to
get a hand-out, sit on them and do nothing, or you
can use them to get a serious grip on yourself.

But when you've put yourself in your
own good hands, don't forget to give yourself
an occasional pat on the back.

Say, 'Well done, pussycat, you're doing okay!'

Superannuation is what we get paid
for being bored for thirty years

It seems to me we're obsessed with having things. We put ourselves in debt for thirty years in order to own a house. We work at thankless jobs we hate for thirty years in order to have sufficient money to retire with security and to die in absolute obscurity.

There is another way. The idea is to dream up the things you want to do and then make them happen.

Life is not about *having* things, life is about *doing* things.

Doing things usually has a rewarding result. You either make more money than you need without being bored in the process, or you discover that you don't really need all that fiscal security to live happily ever after.

You also die smiling.

Putting a dream into action

Nothing in the world can take the place of persistence. Talent will not; nothing is more common than unsuccessful men with talent. Genius will not; unrewarded genius is almost a proverb. Education will not; the world is full of educated derelicts. Persistence and determination alone are omnipotent. The slogan 'Press On' has solved and always will solve the problems of the human race.

Calvin Coolidge

A recipe to dream

one dream.
Dream it in detail. Put it into your own hands. See its
final outcome clearly in your mind. Mix it with a little
effort and add a generous portion of self-discipline.

Flavour it with a wholesome pinch of ambition. Stir briskly with confidence until the mixture becomes clear, the doubt separated from the resolution. Bake at an even temperature in a moderate mind until the dream rises and is firm to the touch. Decorate with individuality. Cut into generous portions and serve with justifiable pride.

Approached in this manner, life is a piece of cake.

Good luck.

Good luck is what almost always comes to those who use the recipe for dreaming and, having dreamed their dream, never, never give up until they have it.

Never attempt to write a book until you've written one hundred long letters to ten true friends.

Why do all folk songs sound the same?

if you sit down to write for posterity, determined to leave your footprint on the sands of time, just remember, the tide comes in and the tide goes out every day.

being famous isn't all it's cracked up to be, but it's definitely better than not being famous.

Colleen McCullough, the world famous Australian writer, claims she always wanted to be famous, although she didn't much mind what she became famous for.

When we chop down the tall poppies
only the weeds remain.

Some people enjoy being miserable.
Some people enjoy the frustration of trying
to comfort them. It is always best to leave them
to themselves as both are engaged in a pointless
exercise in self-indulgence.

Teach your kids early the love of reading and in this way you will nourish their imaginations. This is the greatest gift, after love, that a parent can bestow upon a growing mind.

If you read one good book a month to your kids you will do more for their education than the entire education system will achieve in ten years.

I have a theory that when we are stopped by law from openly telling racial jokes we will risk becoming racist. Laughing, the each about the other, seems a splendid way to clear the air. Hiding our fear of foreigners is the best way I know to nurture the darker side of jingoism.

Why are most men perfectly happy to have a regular beer or ten, laugh, play, get drunk, womanise and spend considerable leisure time with their mates, but, when faced with a personal or family crisis, are unwilling or unable to share or show their grief to mates or to give or take comfort from each other?

Man's

greatest inheritance is the gift of speech.

The gift of words is the gift of imagination.

Each of us has been
designed for one of two immortal functions, as either
a storyteller or as a cross-legged listener to tales of
wonder, love and daring. When we cease to tell or
listen, then we no longer exist as people.
Dead men tell no tales.